All About the Body

By Joanne Sinclair

CELEBRATION PRESS
Pearson Learning Group

Contents

About Your Body

We all look different on the outside. For example, a body can be male or female. It can be tall or short. On the inside, our bodies look the same. All bodies have the same **systems** to keep us alive and healthy. These systems work together to make the amazing machine called the human body.

There are four sections in this book. The colored border on each page tells you which section you are reading.

- Section one tells about parts of the body that protect you.

- Section two explains how certain body parts help you move.

- Section three describes the body parts that make your five senses work.

- Section four shows how your body takes care of itself to keep you healthy.

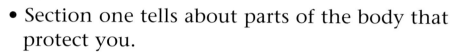

Our Amazing Bodies

Everything in our bodies is made of tiny **cells**. A cell is so tiny that you need a microscope to see it. There are more than 100 trillion cells in the human body. Cells group together to form a **tissue**. Each type of cell has its own special job to do to keep your body alive.

Skin

Skin covers your entire body and holds it together. It protects you from heat, cold, water, germs, and the Sun's rays. Your skin has sensors. They help you feel **texture** and temperature.

Skin is made of two layers. The top layer is a waterproof shield. The inner layer contains blood vessels, sweat glands, and nerve endings.

Your skin is a waterproof barrier.

Cross Section of the Skin

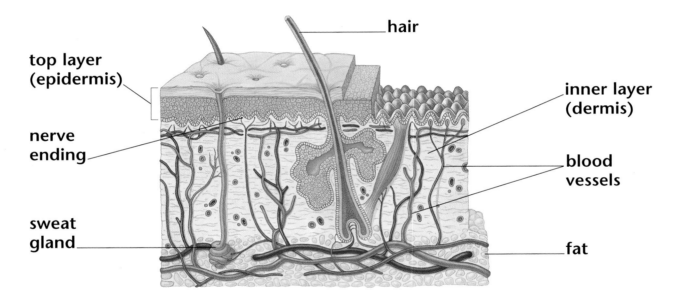

top layer (epidermis)

hair

inner layer (dermis)

nerve ending

blood vessels

sweat gland

fat

Our Amazing Bodies

The skin on your fingertips is covered with a pattern of tiny ridges. These ridges leave marks called fingerprints. No two people have the same pattern of fingerprints.

whorl   loop   arch

Which pattern is most like your fingerprint?

Hair and Nails

Hair and nails grow from the skin. Hair helps keep you warm. Nails protect the sensitive tips of the fingers and toes. Hair and nails contain a hard material called keratin. It doesn't hurt when you cut your hair or nails. This is because they are made of dead cells. The living and growing parts of your hair and nails are under your skin.

Hair on the head grows less than ½ inch every month.

A fingernail grows about ¼ inch every month.

Different Colors
Skin and hair come in many different colors and shades.

5

Skeleton and Bones

You wouldn't be able to stand up without bones. More than 200 bones join together to make your **skeleton**. Your skeleton supports your body's weight and gives it shape. It also protects your **organs** and allows you to move. Bones are made partly of nonliving material. They are also made of living, growing cells. These cells help broken bones grow back together.

An Inside Look

X-rays are used to photograph your bones. In this special photo, you can see the bones of a lower leg and foot.

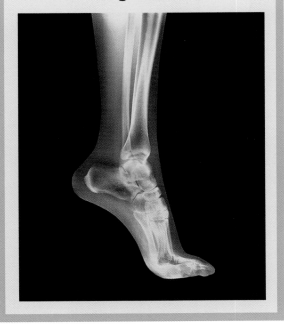

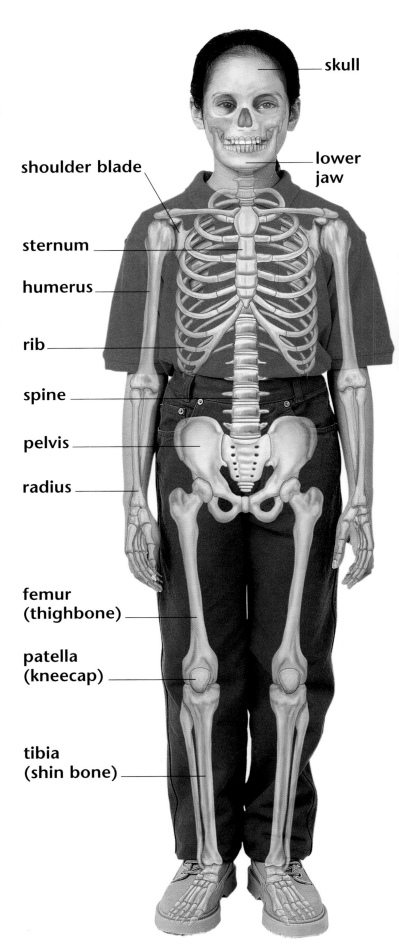

skull

lower jaw

shoulder blade

sternum

humerus

rib

spine

pelvis

radius

femur (thighbone)

patella (kneecap)

tibia (shin bone)

6

Joints and Ligaments

The place where two bones come together is called a joint. Ligaments hold bones together at joints. Your skeleton would not be able to bend, twist, and turn without joints.

The hinge joints in your elbows and knees allow your bones to move forward and backward.

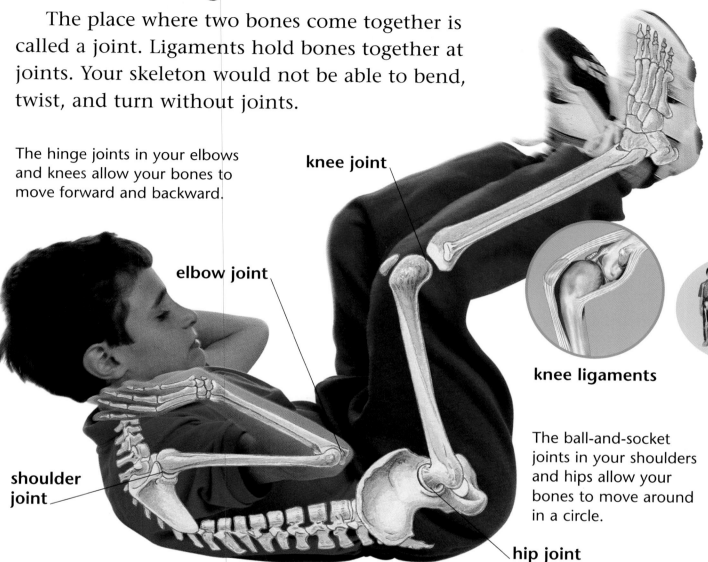

knee joint

elbow joint

shoulder joint

knee ligaments

The ball-and-socket joints in your shoulders and hips allow your bones to move around in a circle.

hip joint

Our Amazing Bodies

There are twenty-seven bones in your hand and wrist. Joints connect all these bones. You can move your hand and wrist in many different ways.

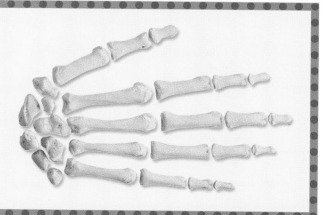

Muscles

The human body has more than 600 muscles. Each has its own shape, size, and function. Muscles help body parts move.

You have control of some muscles, like the ones in your arm. They are called voluntary muscles. You also have muscles that work without you thinking about them. They are called involuntary muscles. These muscles line your throat, stomach, **intestines**, and other organs. The heart is also made of involuntary muscle.

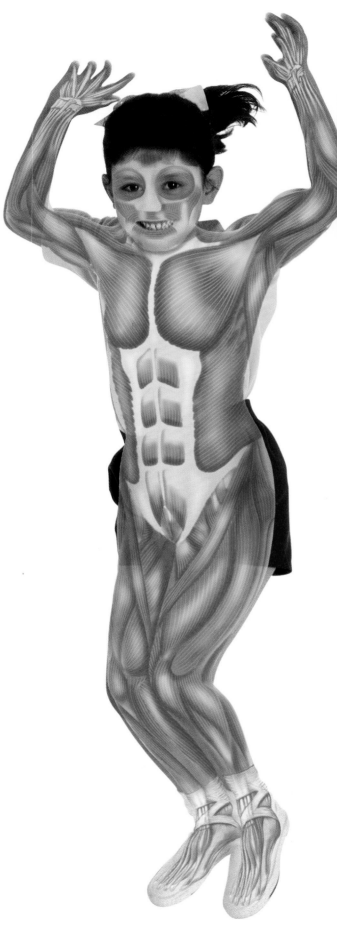

Our Amazing Bodies

More than forty muscles in your face pull on your skin to make your face move. It takes more muscles to frown than to smile. So give your face a break and smile!

Muscles are made of thin fibers. They pull on bones to make them move. Most muscles are attached to bones by cords called tendons.

Muscles often work in pairs. The biceps and triceps arm muscles are one example. As the biceps gets shorter and pulls to bend your arm, the triceps relaxes. Then the triceps gets shorter to straighten your arm. The biceps relaxes while this happens.

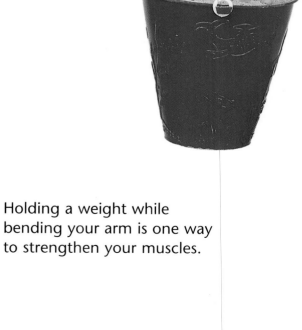

triceps

biceps

Holding a weight while bending your arm is one way to strengthen your muscles.

The Brain and Nervous System

Your brain is the control center of your body. You use your brain to think, feel, and remember. Your brain works with your **nerves** to control all of your actions.

The nervous system is made up of nerves, the brain, and the spinal cord. Nerves connect different parts of the body with the brain and spinal cord. They carry messages between the brain and all parts of the body. Your brain receives and sends billions of messages a day through the body's network of nerves.

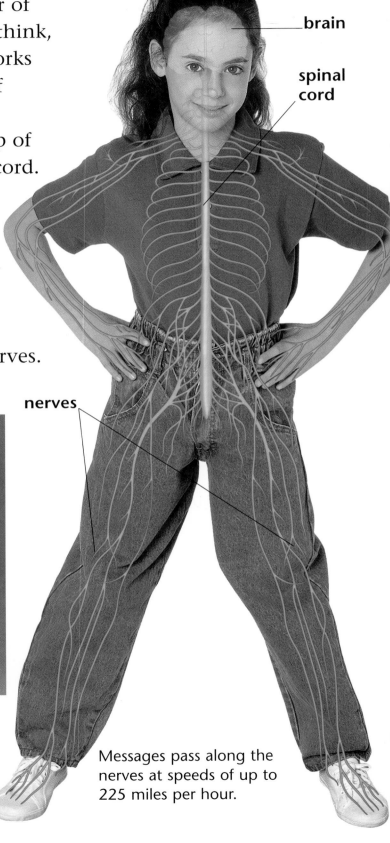

brain

spinal cord

nerves

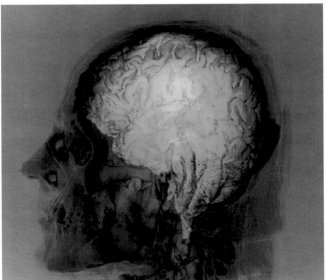

This three-dimensional scan shows what the brain looks like inside the skull.

Messages pass along the nerves at speeds of up to 225 miles per hour.

The main part of your brain is called the cerebrum. It is divided into two parts called hemispheres. Each half of the brain controls certain activities in most people. The right side of the brain controls creative activities such as drawing, painting, and music. The left side of the brain controls speaking, reading, and writing. It also controls problem solving and maths. Both sides of the brain usually work together.

Cerebrum

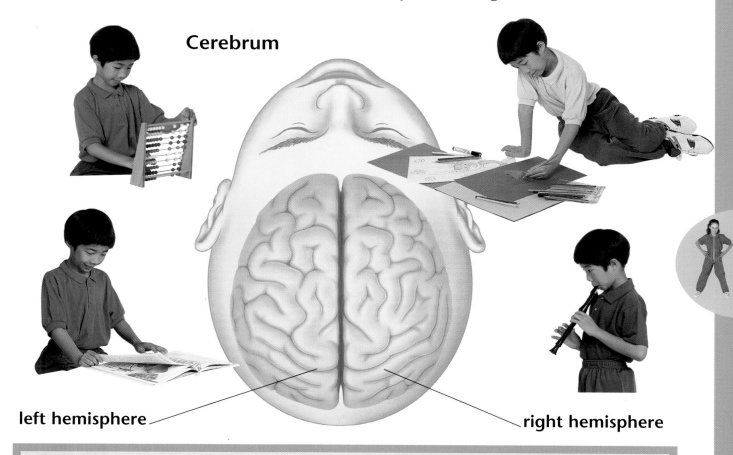

left hemisphere

right hemisphere

Inside the Brain
Different parts of the brain do different jobs. Your cerebrum controls your thinking. Your cerebellum controls your muscles and balance. Your brain stem controls actions you do without thinking, such as breathing.

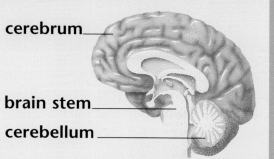

cerebrum

brain stem

cerebellum

Touch

You have millions of tiny touch sensors all over your skin. These help you to feel everything from a light touch to a painful scratch. These touch sensors send messages to your brain about what you are feeling.

The skin on your fingertips is very sensitive. It has many sensors close together. When you can't see, your sense of touch can help you identify objects.

One type of sensor in your hands is a heat sensor. These sensors can warn you about danger. If you touch something hot, you will move your hand before you get burned.

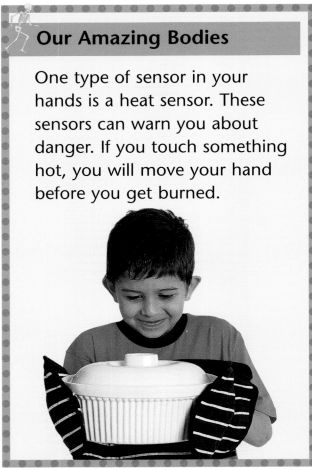

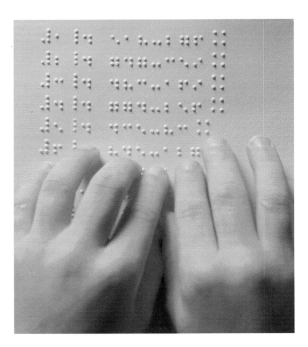

Many people who cannot see learn to read with their fingertips. They use a special alphabet made of raised dots called Braille.

A cat's fur feels soft to touch.

Taste and Smell

Your sense of taste comes from the thousands of tiny taste buds on your tongue. Your sense of smell comes from special cells inside your nose. Without smell and taste, you might miss some wonderful experiences. These senses also warn you about dangers such as rotten food and smoke from a fire.

What would life be like without the scent of a rose or the taste of pizza?

Working Together

Your sense of smell and taste work together. This is why it is hard to taste food when you have a cold. Try tasting apple juice and orange juice while holding your nose. You can probably tell that they are both sweet. You may not be able to tell which one is apple and which one is orange.

Eyes and Sight

Your eyes tell you about the size, shape, color, and location of everything around you. The colored part of the eye is a muscle called the iris. In the middle of the iris is a black spot called the pupil. Your pupil is a hole that lets light into your eye.

When light shines in through the **cornea**, it passes through the pupil. Then the lens focuses the light onto the **retina** to form a picture. Light hits sensors in the retina. Then the sensors send a message to the brain through the **optic nerve**. The brain receives the message and makes a picture in your mind.

Cross Section of the Eye

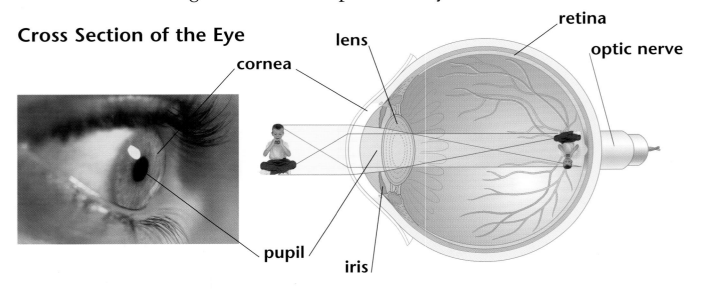

retina

lens

optic nerve

cornea

pupil

iris

Our Amazing Bodies

Your pupils act like windows between your brain and the world outside. They change size to let in more or less light. When the lights are low, the iris opens wide to make the pupil large. This lets more light into the eye. When the lights are bright, the iris closes to make the pupil small. Then less light can enter the eye.

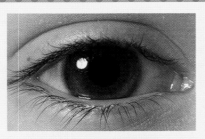

Ears and Hearing

Your ears let you hear a variety of sounds every day. To hear, the **pinna** and ear canal carry sound waves into the eardrum. When the sound waves hit the eardrum, it vibrates. The vibrations pass through the bones of the middle ear to the inner ear. Nerves in the inner ear send messages to the brain.

The inner ear also helps keep you balanced. It sends signals to the brain about head and body movements. The brain sends messages back to the muscles to keep us standing up.

Sign Language
Many people have hearing problems or cannot hear at all. They can learn sign language so that they can communicate.

Cutaway of the Ear

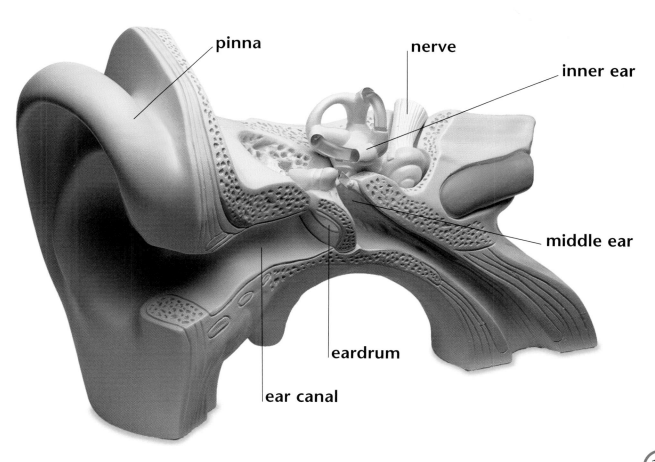

pinna

nerve

inner ear

middle ear

eardrum

ear canal

Blood, Heart, and Circulation

Your heart and blood vessels make up your circulatory system. Your heart is a powerful muscle that is about the size of your fist. It pumps blood around your body through long tubes called blood vessels.

There are three kinds of blood vessels. These are the arteries, veins, and capillaries. Arteries carry the blood away from the heart. Veins bring blood back to the heart. Capillaries connect the arteries and veins. Blood passes through the capillaries and carries oxygen and **nutrients** to all the cells in the body.

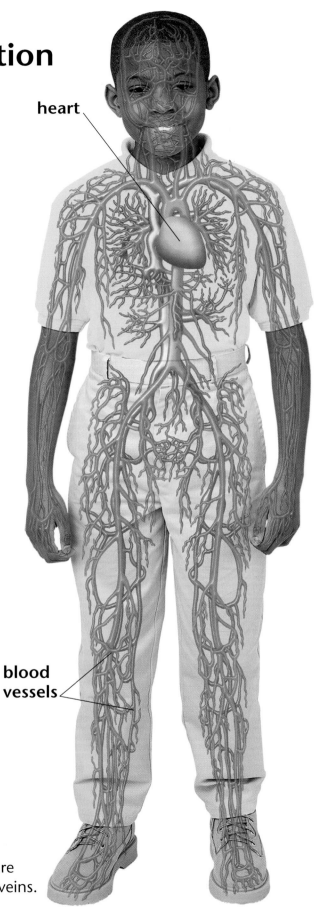

heart

blood vessels

In this diagram, red blood vessels are arteries and blue blood vessels are veins.

Our Amazing Bodies

In this special X-ray photograph, you can see the veins and capillaries in the hand. Imagine you could stretch out all your blood vessels from end to end. They would wind almost three times around the world.

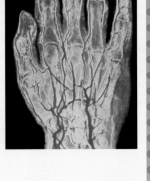

The two sides of your heart have different jobs. The right side of the heart receives blood from the veins. This blood has little oxygen. The heart pumps the blood to the lungs. There, the blood picks up oxygen. Blood flows into the left side of the heart from the lungs. Then the heart pumps it through arteries to the body.

As blood passes along the arteries, it creates a beat. This is called a pulse. You can feel your pulse by placing two fingers on the inside of your wrist, just below your thumb.

Cross Section of the Heart

right side of the heart

left side of the heart

vein

artery

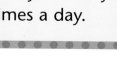

Our Amazing Bodies

Your heart beats about 100,000 times a day. Your body has about 8 pints of blood. A drop of blood goes around your body more than 1,000 times a day.

17

Lungs and Breathing

Your body needs oxygen to stay alive. You get oxygen by breathing in air through your mouth and nose. The air goes down your **windpipe** and into your lungs. The oxygen passes into the blood. It is then carried to the rest of your body. The blood picks up a gas called carbon dioxide from the cells. Then the blood is pumped back into your lungs. When you breathe out, the carbon dioxide leaves your body.

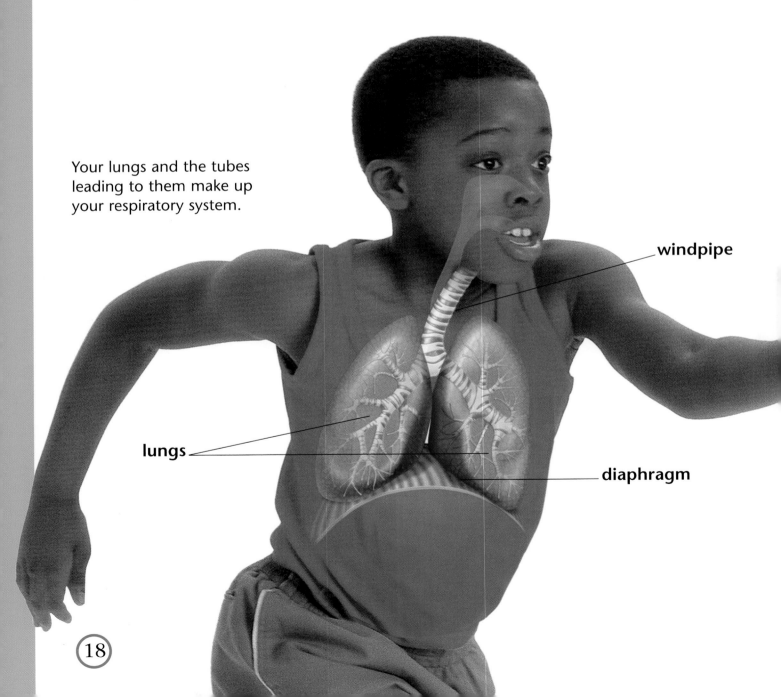

Your lungs and the tubes leading to them make up your respiratory system.

windpipe

lungs

diaphragm

Your lungs fill with air and empty out with the help of muscles. The diaphragm (Dy-uh-fram) is a large muscle between your chest and stomach. It works with the rib muscles to make you breathe. Sometimes the diaphragm twitches for a minute or two. This is what causes hiccups.

Your lungs and diaphragm help you blow up a balloon.

Our Amazing Bodies

Sneezing helps your body to remove dust or germs from your airways. The blast of air from a sneeze pushes dust and germs out of your nose. Air travels down your nose at more than 100 miles per hour.

Eating and Digestion

The food you eat gives you energy and nutrients. You need food for your body to stay active and to grow. Your digestive system breaks down the food. Then your body's cells can use it as fuel.

Our Amazing Bodies

Your teeth tear, chew, and break up food into small pieces. This makes food easier to swallow and digest. You start out with a set of twenty teeth. At about six years old, you begin to lose them. One by one, adult teeth grow in to make your second set. Most adults have thirty-two teeth. Brushing your teeth every day can help keep them healthy.

What happens after you take a bite of a sandwich? Any food or drink you swallow makes a long trip through your body. Muscles push the food down the **esophagus** (ah-SAHF-u-gus) and into your stomach. The food is mashed up into a thick, soupy mixture. As it flows through your intestines, nutrients from the food go into your blood. The parts of food that your body does not need leave your body as waste.

It can take up to 24 hours to digest one meal.

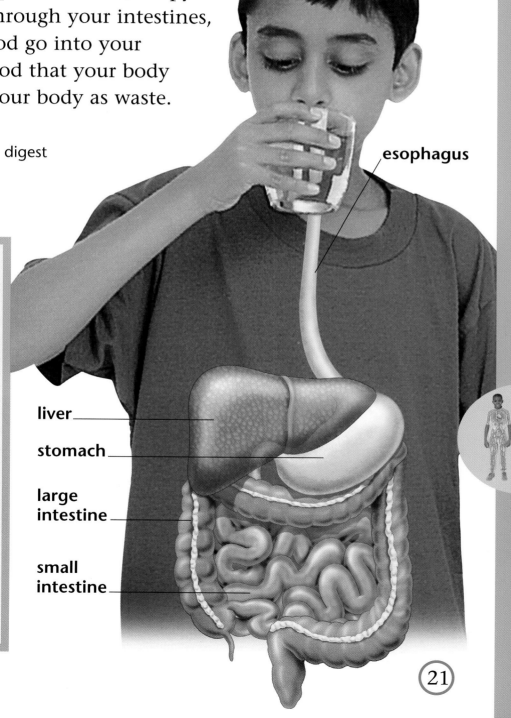

esophagus

liver

stomach

large intestine

small intestine

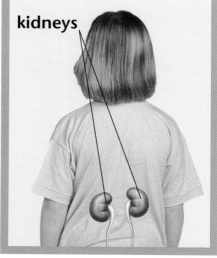

The Kidneys' Job
Your kidneys help remove liquid wastes and extra water that your body does not need.

kidneys

21

The Body Team

The body is made up of many, many parts. Each one has an important job to do. Some body parts help you move around. Other body parts control your senses. They help you take in information from the world around you. Still other parts help your body grow and stay healthy. All of your organs and systems work together like a team to make you move, breathe, and think. The human body is truly amazing!

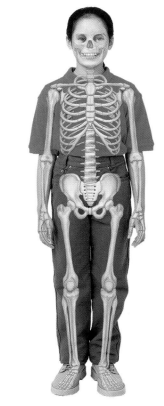

Your skeleton supports your body and gives it shape.

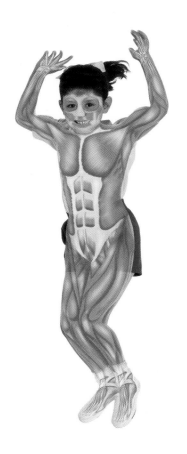

Your muscles help body parts move.

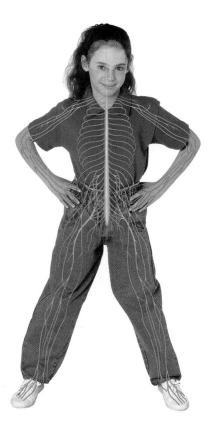

Nerves carry messages between your brain and all parts of your body.

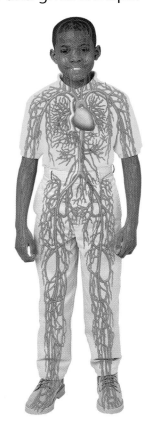

Arteries and veins carry blood around your body.

Glossary

cells   tiny living units of all plants and animals

cornea   the clear outer part of the eye that covers the pupil and iris

esophagus   the tube that carries food from the throat to the stomach

intestines   the parts of the body that digest food and absorb nutrients

nerves   the parts of the body that carry messages to and from the brain

nutrients   substances found in food that the body uses for energy, growth, and repair

optic nerve   the main nerve that sends messages from the eye to the brain

organs   the parts of an animal or plant that have some special purpose

pinna   the part of the ear outside the head

retina   the inside part of the eye that reacts to light

skeleton   the framework of bones which supports the body and carries its weight

systems   groups of body parts that work together to perform jobs

texture   the look and feel of something

tissue   a group of cells that look alike and work together to do a certain job

windpipe   the tube that carries air to the lungs

Index